Made in United States
North Haven, CT
19 August 2022

22894841R00055